AGGRESSOR aircraft ★

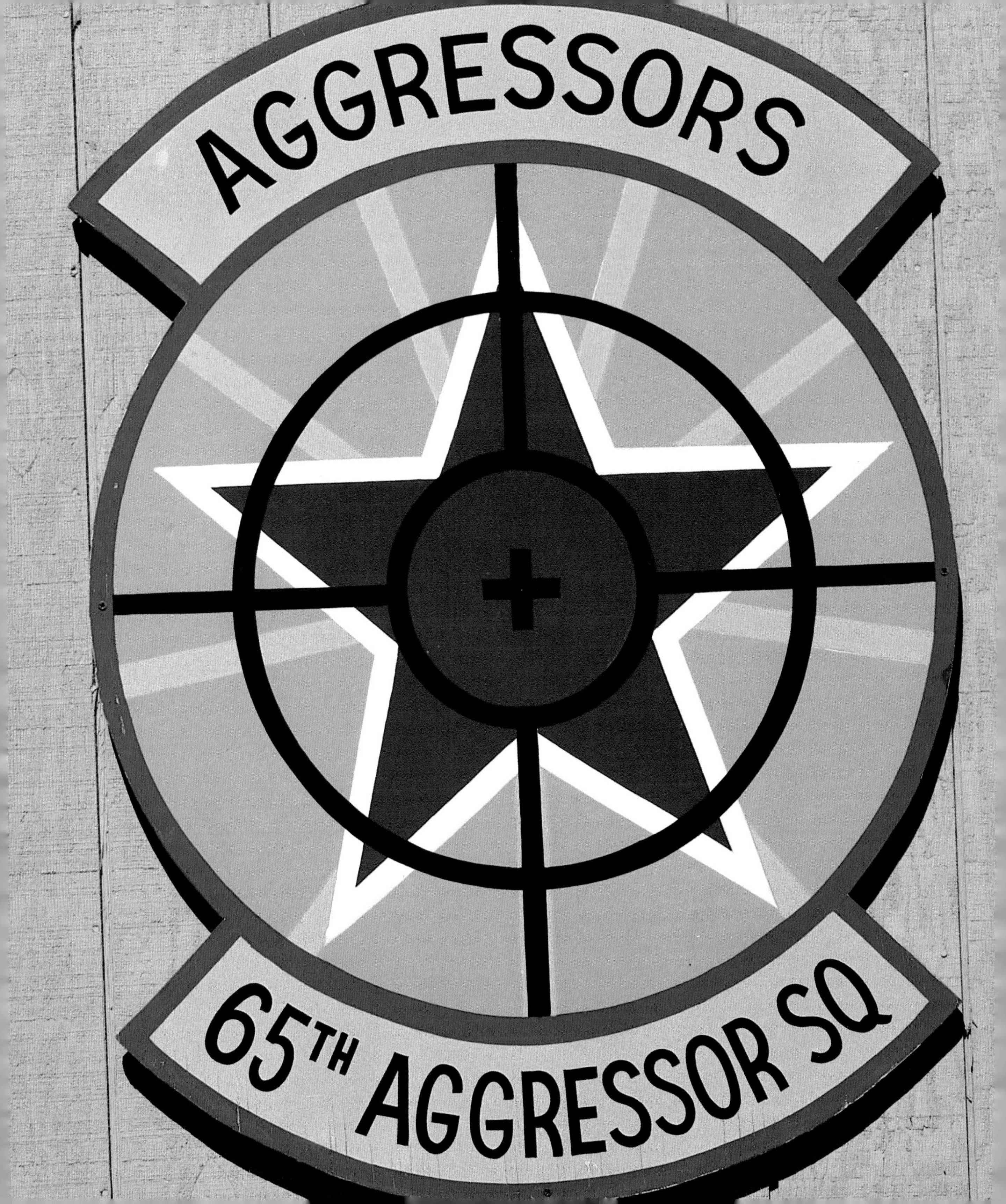
AGGRESSORS
65TH AGGRESSOR SQ

AGGRESSOR aircraft ☆

Chuck Stewart

OSPREY AEROSPACE

ACKNOWLEDGEMENTS

Most of the photos in this book would have been impossible to obtain without the generous assistance of two groups of people. First, the men in the aggressor units whose understanding and initiative helped clear the numerous obstacles to flightline photography: Lt Mike Good of VF-126, Lt Chet Sublett of the 'Desert Hawks', Capt Dick Thomas of VMFT-401, and a good friend, MSgt Rich Blaich at Nellis AFB. And second, the contributing photographers, whose excellent work appears throughout the book: Aggressor Aircraft would not have been possible without the help of Michael Grove, Gary James, Craig Kaston, Ben Knowles, Ray Leader, Iain Macpherson, Joe Michaels, Paul Minert, Brian Rodgers, Bob Shane, Chuck Stewart, Sr, Bruce Trombecky, and Jim Tunney.

To them and all the others who helped, thanks!

Published in 1990 by Osprey Publishing Limited
59 Grosvenor Street, London W1X 9DA

© Chuck Stewart 1990

British Library Cataloguing in Publication Data

Stewart, Chuck
    Aggressor aircraft—(colour series).
    1. American military forces. Military aircraft, history.
    Camouflage & markings
    I. Title
    358.4183

    ISBN 0 85045 986 9

Editor Tony Holmes
Designed by Paul Kime
Printed in Hong Kong

Right An unusually drab VF-45 'Mongoose' taxies out at NAS Fallon. The 'AD' tailcodes on all 'Blackbird' aircraft identify the fleet and air wing to which they belong. 'A' indicates Atlantic fleet and 'N' the Pacific. The 'D' indicates Light Attack Wing One, whose units are shore-based at Key West, Oceana and Cecil (*Grove*)

Front cover Flying lead in this echelon-left formation of TA-4Js is former VF-45 boss CDR Jim 'Boink' Ryan, and AMS-1 Mark McCabe, along for the incentive ride of a lifetime. Flying wing in 'red 13', BuNo 154327, is LCDR Tom 'Maggot' McInvale (*Trombecky*)

Back cover Down in the weeds, a 'Desert Hawk' crew pause briefly whilst they plan the next run in on 'enemy' armoured positions

For a catalogue of all books published by Osprey Aerospace please write to:

**The Marketing Manager, Consumer Catalogue Department
Osprey Publishing Ltd, 59 Grosvenor Street, London, W1X 9DA**

Introduction

Although the first squadron was not created until 1969, today's aggressor units actually had their origins during World War 2 when pilots like Charles Lindbergh visited frontline air bases in both theatres to demonstrate an aircraft's maximum performance capability, as well as the latest combat manoeuvres. The idea, as it still is today, was to give American pilots the experience and advantage of realistic training, the edge that could make the critical difference in aerial combat.

When the US Navy's air-to-air kill ratio dropped from 14:1 during World War 2 to a very costly and unacceptable 2.3:1 midway through the Vietnam War, it was apparent that a change in pilot training was desperately needed. Captain Frank W Ault was tasked to explore the reasons for the poor kill ratio and make recommendations to triple it as soon as possible. His thorough, year-long study contained some 240 recommended changes to the Navy's fighter weapons programme. One of these resulted in the creation of the Navy Fighter Weapons School, Top Gun, in March 1969, the first of the true aggressor units. Another was the development of the first Air Combat Manoeuvering Range (later, 'TACTS' – tactical air combat training systems) and the entire concept of dissimilar air combat training (DACT) for the fleet by special 'adversary' squadrons.

The Air Force was experiencing the same disappointing kill ratio in Vietnam and commissioned its own study to determine the reasons and possible cures. The 'Red Baron Study', like the Navy's Ault report, concluded that experience in simulated combat scenarios dramatically improved a pilot's performance and chance of survival in actual combat. From this conclusion was born the concept of the 'Red Flag' combat training exercises and the special adversary units that would conduct them.

With the immediate improvement in the Vietnam kill ratio that followed the establishment of these special units, it was clear that aggressors were here to stay.

When most of us think of aggressor aircraft, the names Top Gun and 'Red Flag' come to mind and quickly sum up the subject. However, no image could provide a less complete picture of aggressor units in the US. The Navy alone has a dozen aggressor squadrons, the Air Force a total of two, the Marines three, the Army one, and even the Department of Defense has a special aggressor unit. This book concentrates its coverage on the 'major' aggressor units of each service, as these are the most typical and have the widest aircraft types, including the very latest USAF F-16s, and it would be impossible to include a photo of every different colour scheme. As many as possible are included, but for each that is, there are countless variations (especially on Navy aircraft) that continue to change every time an aeroplane undergoes a maintenance inspection or overhaul.

US AIR FORCE

26th Aggressor Squadron (AS) Kadena AB, the Philippines (now deactivated)
64th AS – Nellis AFB, Nevada (now deactivated)
65th AS – Nellis AFB, Nevada (now deactivated)
527th AS – Alconbury, England (now deactivated)

US MARINE CORPS

VMFT-401 'Snipers' – MCAS Yuma, Arizona
MALS-24 (Maintenance Aviation Logistics Squadron) 'Bandits' –MCAS Kaneohe Bay, Hawaii
MALS-31 'Aggressors' – MCAS Beaufort, South Carolina

US ARMY

'C' Company, 3/159th Assault Helicopter Battalion, 'Desert Hawks' – Barstow-Daggett, California

US DEPARTMENT OF DEFENSE

DTESA (Defense Test & Support Evaluation Agency), part of the DOD's Operational Test & Evaluation Office – Kirtland AFB, New Mexico

US NAVY

NFWS (Navy Fighter Weapons School) 'Top Gun' – NAS Miramar, California
VF-43 'Challengers' – NAS Oceana, Virginia
VF-45 'Blackbirds' – NAS Key West, Florida
VF-126 'Bandits' – NAS Miramar, California
VFA-127 'Cylons' – NAS Fallon, Nevada
VC-1 'Blue Alii' – NAS Barber's Point, Hawaii
VC-5 'Checkertails' – NAS Cubi Point, the Philippines
VC-8 'Redtails' – NS Roosevelt Roads, Puerto Rico
VC-10 'Challengers' – NS Guantanamo Bay, Cuba
VFC-12 'Fighting Omars' – NAS Oceana, Virginia
VFC-13 'Saints' – NAS Miramar, California
OMD (Operational Maintenance Division) 'Rangers' – NAS Dallas, Texas

Contents

Above 'Red 32', on display at the main gate at RAF Alconbury, represents the end of an era. After 16 years in service, the Air Force replaced the F-5s in its aggressor squadrons with F-16Cs. Eight 527th AS Tigers went to VFA-127 at NAS Fallon, the others to the Davis-Monthan boneyard and foreign buyers like Brazil. The 527th left RAF Alconbury, its home since the unit was activated in June 1976, for RAF Bentwaters in September 1988

Heinemann's hellraiser

Right Stationed at NAS Key West, VF-45's A-4s wear some of the most colourful aggressor camouflage schemes. This flight of four heads for the 'Whisky 174' warning area near the Dry Tortugas Islands, west of the Florida Keys. Flying the TA-4s are Lt Roger 'Muff' Dadiomoff in 'red 06' and Lt Silas 'Cylon' Hart in 'red 02'. The A-4Es are piloted by LCDR John 'Toons' Looney in 'red 12' and LCDR Lynn 'Porky' Baughman in 'red 10' (*Trombecky*)

Below VF-45 was first assigned DACT missions in August 1976 while still based at NAS Cecil Field flying TA-4Js. Four years after relocating to Key West in 1980, they were designated an actual aggressor squadron and tasked with adversary training for east coast fighter, strike and attack pilots. 'Blackbird' two-seater, BuNo 153471, is flown by Lt 'Cylon' Hart (*Trombecky*)

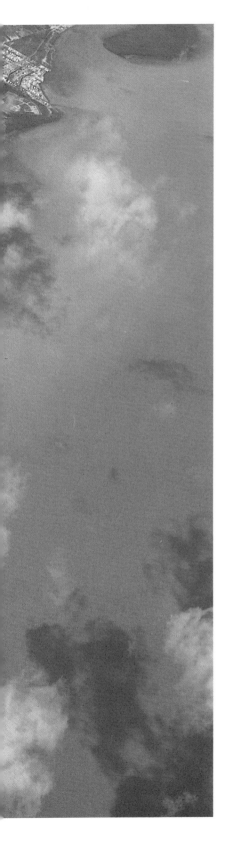

Left Demonstrating the effectiveness of their camouflage, a VF-45 two-ship banks overhead the three crossing runways of NAS Key West (*Trombecky*)

Above VF-45 XO, CDR John 'Turkey' Ward, goes inverted for a simulated MiG-17 guns shot as his prey bugs out. The TA-4J versus F/A-18 tussle is taking place in Key West's 'Whiskey 174' area, February 1986 (*Trombecky*)

Right One of VF-43's four TA-4Js, BuNo 158136, photographed at home station following a typical Florida afternoon shower. Unlike the Air Force, Navy aggressor units change the Soviet 'Bort' numbers on their aircraft quiet frequently, '01', for example, originally being '15' (*Kaston*)

Below One of the cleanest and most colourful aircraft ever to fly with VF-43 was this A-4F photographed in April 1976. This scheme was a welcome change from the weathered blue/grey camouflage the 'Challengers' have used exclusively since they were tasked as the adversary training unit for Atlantic Fleet fighter squadrons in 1973. Like the 'Mongoose', the A-4F 'Super Fox' is powered by the Pratt & Whitney P-8 and is a supreme dogfighter at low level (*Michaels*)

Left VF-45's eight A-4Es are amongst the oldest in the Navy's aggressor inventory. Flying 'red 12', BuNo 149653, is LCDR 'Toons' Looney, and in 'red 10', BuNo 151064, is LCDR 'Porky' Baughman (*Trombecky*)

Above Two of the first Navy units to be assigned adversary missions were VF-121, the former Pacific Fleet F-4 RAG at Miramar, and a Key West detachment of Oceana-based VF-101, 121's Atlantic Fleet counterpart. Both flew Phantom IIs and later, Skyhawks. VF-101's RAG mission, and its Key West aggressor det, were transferred to VF-171 until 1984 when the F-4 was finally deposed by the F-14 and the squadron was deactivated. The colourful crest on this A-4E, photographed in March 1980, confirms that it belongs to VF-171 Det Key West (*Tunney*)

A flight of VA-127 TA-4Js over the
Sierra Nevadas, February 1986. 'Red
15' is flown by Lts Carl 'Cach'
Abelein and Paul 'Po' Pohlmeyer,
whilst 'red 16' is piloted by then-CO,
Capt Mike 'Hawk' Sullivan
(*Trombecky*)

Right An impressive cast of 'characters' mans this diamond formation of 'Cylon' A-4s over the Nevada desert near Yuma in Jaunary 1983. Flying lead in 'red 01', an A-4F, is then-CO, CDR 'Caesar' DeCarl; left wing is then-XO, CDR 'Booger' Valovich and Lt 'Ezzard' Charles; right wing in 'red 05', Lt 'TD' Durkin and LCDR 'Padre' McNulty; trail in 'red 10' is LCDR 'JR' Goddard and Lt 'Whopper' Barnes (*Trombecky*)

Below Chief 'Cylon', 'Caesar' DeCarl, takes a two-ship down for a closer look at things near Yuma (*Trombecky*)

Opposite above One of the 12 Skyhawks on VFA-127's books is this TA-4J, BuNo 154334. The move to Fallon was extremely beneficial for the 'Cylons' as it made them the only full squadron based there and gave them easy access to the most modern TACTS range operating in the US. It also provided them with a steady stream of customers, as most fleet carrier air wings work up at Fallon each year

Opposite below The VFA-127 equivalent of the Air Force 'snake' camouflage pattern is worn by this TA-4F. The 'Cylons' received their first TA-4Fs in September 1966, initiating a change of mission from instrument training to A-4 replacement training and, eventually, ACM for all Pacific Fleet light attack squadrons

Above Relatively few A-4Fs entered adversary service still wearing their dorsal avionics humps and fin-mounted ECM pods, this 'Super Fox', BuNo 154992, being one of the few. An ex-Marine aircraft, it carries the old VA-127 emblem on the tail, a MiG-19 silhouette inside a red star and gunsight circle.

Above Lts 'Po' Pohlmeyer and Marvin 'Otis' Wade in 'red 14', BuNo 158465, in February 1986 (*Trombecky*)

Right A trio of VF-126 Skyhawks over the Salton Sea near NAS El Centro, California, in May 1984. Flying the TA-4J adorned with five MiG kills is then-'Bandit' CO, CDR Randy 'Duke' Cunningham, the Navy's only Vietnam ace. Flying 'red 21', an A-4F in a camouflage scheme based on that worn by Libyan MiG-23s, is Lt 'Thor' Jensen. Flying lead in 'red 22', which sports the old style 'Fighting 126' unit emblem on its tail, is Lt 'G-Man' Mosley (*Trombecky*)

A pair of VF-126 TA-4Js in Air Force style 'ghost' camouflage on patrol over the Yuma ACM range in October 1983. Flying lead in 'red 12', BuNo 153513, is then - 'Bandit' CO, CDR Dave Carey. His wingmen in 'red 07', BuNo 152858, are Lt Brian Tyndall and ENS Dwight Jenkins (*Trombecky*)

Left Though VF-126 flew both T-38s and F-5s, the most popular, plentiful and long-lived aircraft on its rolls is the venerable A-4. Here, a colourful line-up of VF-126 Skyhawks is seen on the Miramar ramp

Above The space devoted to the VF-126 paint store must be considerable!

Overleaf Six years and some 1800 gruelling ACM-hours later, BuNo 154181 is still flying, but hardly looks like a jewel anymore. Nevertheless, this seemingly worn-out old warhorse continues to beat up over-confident Tomcat and Hornet pilots throughout the Pacific Fleet

Left This trio of TA-4Js demonstrates the 'Bandit' penchant for oddball colour schemes. 'Double Nuts', BuNo 152861, wears the rare A-4 scheme of overall anodized silver; '02' BuNo 154288, wears a combination of Israeli-style pastels; and '04', BuNo 153518, wears an unusual progression of grey/greens

Above The distinctive lengthened nose of the A-4E houses the APN-153(V) navigation radar, a rather austere system by today's standards

Left The tan/olive/rust scheme on this TA-4J is an exact copy of the tactical camouflage worn by Russian MiG-21s (*Macpherson*)

Above Lt Mike 'Johnny B' Good, VF-126's Public Affairs officer and aggressor extraordinaire, shows off the 'Bandit' colours in front of one of the squadron's Skyhawks

Above This rear view of 'red 32' shows some of the A-4's aerodynamic features: the all-moving tailplane and the row of vortex generators along the trailing edges of the wings which increase the effectiveness of aileron control

Opposite above Top Gun's oldest A-4 is BuNo 149656, which, back in 1974, was the mount of Lt Randy 'Duke' Cunningham. Flying F-4Js, he and his RIO, Lt JG Willie 'Irish' Driscoll, were the only Navy aces of the Vietnam War. Both Cunningham and Driscoll attended the first Top Gun class in March 1969 and returned as instructors after their tours in Vietnam. This green scheme has been worn by a Top Gun A-4 for ten years

Opposite below LCDR Brian 'Beef' Flannery, a VF-126 'Bandit', poses beside a Top Gun A-4E. On his left shoulder he wears the coveted Top Gun patch, indicating that he, like all fully-qualified aggressor pilots, is a graduate of the Navy Fighter Weapons School

After going through six colour schemes since it first joined Top Gun is 1974, BuNo 150023 now wears this common blue/grey camouflage. The school's second-oldest A-4, it is a battle-damaged Vietnam veteran, but is still able to teach a rookie F-14 jock a thing or two in a dogfight

Left 'Viper's' A-4 awaits its real master, Lt Bob 'Ice' Ffield, outside Miramar's Hangar One. Although some have accumulated almost 30-years of mostly ACM flying, the A-4 more than holds its own against the latest Navy fighters. The 'Mongoose' used by all aggressors is a stripped-down, souped-up version of the A-4E powered by an uprated Pratt & Whitney J52P-8 engine that produces nearly 11,000 pounds of thrust without being afterburner capable. Though it is subsonic, with a 1:1 thrust to weight ratio it can outclimb anything but an F-16, and its tight, high-G turning ability, especially at lower altitudes, makes it a merciless opponent in a dogfight

Below The third aggressor unit stationed at NAS Miramar is VFC-13, the 'Saints'. Designated an adversary squadron in April 1988, they fly 14 TA-4Js and A-4Fs. This freshly painted 'Super Fox', BuNo 154976, wears the unit's brand-new tail emblem and is an ex-VMA-124 bird

Right A TA-4J of VC-1, the 'Blue Alii', on a threat simulation mission high above Hawaii. Based at NAS Barbers Point, Composite Squadron One flies A-4Es and TA-4Js in the adversary role, and CH-53A Sea Stallions as Carrier On board Delivery (COD) transports. The only aggressor squadron operating in the Hawaiian islands, VC-1 supports a wide variety of Navy, Marine and Air National Guard units, as well as units in transit across 'the pond' and TDY for excercises (*Trombecky*)

Below Tasked with providing adversary training for the Corps, Marine Aviation Logistics Squadron (MALS)-31 'Aggressors' fly from MCAS Beaufort, South Carolina. BuNo 154641 is one of five TA-4Fs (and one TA-4J) flown by MALS-31 as adversary support for both Marine Air Group 31 and the Second Air Wing (*Michaels*)

Nautical feline

A two-ship of Top Gun F-5Fs over the Pacific near San Clemente Island. In the lead in 'red 47' are Lts Steve Harden and Mike Galpin, whilst in the wingman's position are Lt Sandy Winnefield and LCDR Mike Denkler. The camouflage on 'black 50', BuNo 160966, is based on the Swedish Air Force zig-zag pattern (*Trombecky*)

Above An early Top Gun F-5. Special markings like the black hawk below the canopy were shortlived, the personal touch being limited to the pilot's callsign on the canopy rail. BuNo 159882 was written-off in a crash in September 1984

Opposite above Not long for this world, BuNo 159879 taxies out at Tinker AFB, Oklahoma, on 12 April 1981. One month later to the day it crashed, and was replaced on the Top Gun roster by a newer F-5E, BuNo 162307

Opposite below A Top Gun F-5E in one of the earliest Navy aggressor schemes, photographed in August 1977. The '03' oversprayed just above the Top Gun emblem on the tail is a remnant of a marking system deleted earlier in the year. BuNo 159880 arrived at Top Gun in 1974 sporting factory-fresh USAF South-east Asian camouflage. It would wear several more schemes before finally being transferred to VFA-127 at Fallon in 1987. In the background is a naval aggressor landmark, the Top Gun hangar, adorned with MiG-21 silhouettes representing actual kills made in Vietnam by Top Gun graduates

VFA-127 CO, CDR Ridge 'Junkyard' Corbin, wanted an aircraft that would help build 'Cylon' esprit de corps and remind people that VFA-127 was the only squadron in the Navy still flying the F-5. This matte-black F-5 has proven to be just the attention-grabber he wanted. 'Red 23', BuNo 160792, came to Fallon from VF-126 at Miramar, where it flew as 'NJ652'

Inset 'Red 23' carries the name of VFA-127's maintenance officer, ENS Theresa 'Tree' Clark, in authentic Cyrillic script on both sides of the cockpit. The F-15 'kill' marking is the result of an ACM victory and is a snub to Air Force Eagle drivers everywhere

Overleaf Not a Hollywood 'MiG-28', though the all-black scheme was inspired by the movie Top Gun. The all-black F-5 is used by VFA-127 as the squadron mascot and also as the regular airshow mount

Right No matter that the F-5 is based on a 33-year-old design and that it is a relatively basic machine in comparison to the Tomcats and Hornets it fights. As this photo shows, it is still incredibly sleek and modern-looking, or in aggressor parlance, it is a 'tits machine'!

Below At about the same time the 'Cylons' were relocating to Fallon, both Top Gun and VF-45 at Key West were transitioning to the F-16N, the best of their F-5Es being transferred to VFA-127 to beef up its A-4 fleet. In late 1988, when Air Force aggressor squadrons also transitioned to F-16s, the 'Cylons' received eight more ex-USAF F-5s, bringing their F-5 fleet up to 16 aircraft

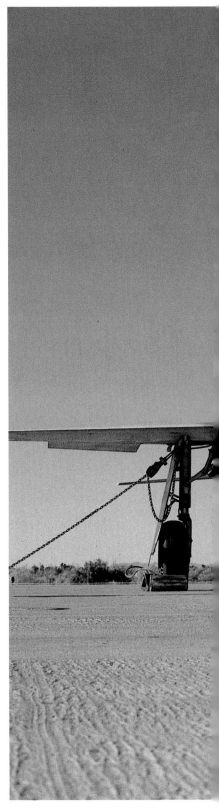

Still wearing the 'ghost' scheme it wore with the 527th AS at RAF Alconbury, 'red 46', s/n 74-1568, bakes on the Fallon ramp in June 1989 (*Grove*)

One of the ex-Nellis F-5s, s/n 74-1564, taxies back from an aborted take-off at
Fallon. Its new camouflage is the same as that applied by Northrop to the F-5Es
sold to the Imperial Iranian, Royal Saudi and other Middle East air forces

A coat of black latex paint and spurious markings converted this pair of NFWS F-5s into 'MiG-28s' for the 1986 Paramount movie, Top Gun. Operating from Miramar, Fallon and Nellis during the summer of 1985, four Es and one F model were used in filming the spectacular dogfight scenes from the movie. LCDR Bob 'Rat' Willard, who served as Top Gun's adviser to the film crew, managed to get 16 Top Gun pilots involved in the 'MiG-28' flying (Grove)

Another Top Gun cast-off is this F-5F undergoing maintenance on a crowded Fallon ramp. BuNo 160965 flew with the NFWS for 10 years, most recently as 'red 47', before joining VFA-127 in October 1987 (*Grove*)

Tiger II, USAF style

An F-5 two-ship holds for departure at Deci in October 1986. The 526th maintained a permanent detachment of six F-5s at the Sardinian base to provide ACM training to all comers. However, because of a budget crunch that cancelled all USAF flying at the Deci ACMI range, and in preparation for the transition to F-16s and the move to RAF Bentwaters, the 527th sat out 1988 at home in England

Left The 'ghost' scheme on this F-5 is the most popular and effective of the various USAF aggressor camouflage schemes. Major Ken Clarke taxies by in 'red 34' , s/n 74-1534

Below The USAF equivalent of Top Gun's legendary Hangar One at Miramar was the adversary tactics building at Nellis AFB, Nevada. Here, the pilot-instructors from the 64th and 65th Aggressor Squadrons developed and conducted the academic portion of their ACM/DACT training mission

A 'new blue' F-5 on the Deci ramp

This F-5E, s/n 74–1563, wears a grey air superiority scheme and unusual blue 'Bort' numbers. Navy and Marine 'Bort' numbers are assigned and changed randomly with no relation to an aeroplane's bureau number. The Air Force, however, uses the last two digits of a plane's actual serial number to create the permanent 'Bort' number for that plane, regardless of paint scheme or reallocation to another aggressor squadron

Opposite Backseater's view as a 64th FWS T-38 rolls hard right to the inverted for a guns shot in a one v one against an F-4E during a 1974 Red Flag exercise at Nellis

Above Following successful DACT trials with F-106s, the Air Force instituted its adversary training programme with the activation of the 64th Fighter Weapons Squadron at Nellis in October 1972, the 65th FWS following in October 1975. Initially, both units were equipped with Air Training Command T-38A, the closest thing in the inventory to the MiG-21. These all-white Talons were quickly repainted in a variety of camouflage schemes based on those of potential adversaries. This T-38, s/n 64-13169, wears the colours known as the 'lizard' scheme and, like most aggressor T-38s, was transferred to the 465th Tactical Fighter Training Squadron, 479th Tactical Training Wing at Holloman AFB after being replaced by F-5Es in 1975. 'Red 69' is shown at Holloman in April 1979, flying with the 465th TFTS and still sporting its aggressor colours

One of two 65th TFTAS F-5s that visited McConnell AFB, Kansas, in May 1981 to provide home station DACT to F-4D crews from the 184th TFG, the Air Force Reserve RTU (replacement training unit). 'Red 65', s/n 74–1514, is sprayed up in the regulation version of the 'snake' camouflage scheme

Left A modified 'pumpkin' scheme adorns this 64th TFTAS F-5 on the David-Monthan ramp in June 1984. 'Red 865', s/n 73–0865, wore a three digit 'Bort' number to avoid being mistaken for 'red 65', s/n 74–1565, the 65th TFTAS CO's mount (*Rogers*)

Below The head-on cross-section of the F-5 is very small, making the aircraft a difficult target to pick up visually. Its size, allied with its extreme agility, made the Tiger II a deadly adversary. The 64th and 65th ASs began winding down their operations with this aircraft in August 1988 with the deactivation and transfer of a dozen F-5s, still in aggressor camouflage, to Brazil. By the first week of April 1989, what had been a 39-plane roster was down to only 18 aircraft. On 7 April 1989, the Nellis F-5s made their last flight as USAF aggressors. One week later, the aircraft were in open storage in Arizona. Thirteen of them were being held at MCAS Yuma to replace VMFT-401's lend-lease F-21 Kfirs, which were to be returned to Israel in September 1989

Above It was 57th FWW policy to identify aggressor squadron aircraft by marking them with different coloured 'Bort' numbers. The 64th AS had red numbers, the 65th AS, blue. Because scheduling and mission requirements dictated pilots fly whatever aircraft was mission-ready at any given time, regardless of squadron, the policy was not strictly followed or enforced (*Minert*)

Left Line-up of 64th AS F-5s which illustrates the various schemes employed by the unit. Within six months of this shot being taken the venerable F-5s had gone forever

Based on the T-38 and F-5A Freedom Fighter, the F-5E featured such aerodynamic improvements as a longer and wider fuselage, a 16-square-foot increase in wing area, and combat manoeuvring flaps. Nonetheless, the Tiger's 26-foot, 8-inch wingspan provided a relatively small wing area with a maximum wing loading of only 133 pounds per square foot. For this reason, the F-5 tended to bleed off speed in tight combat turns and had to rely on its Mach 1.6 speed as its greatest strength. Here, the 64th TFTAS commander's F-5, 'red 64', is being re-armed amid a ramp full of aggressors and visitors, the latter being an F-5B from Williams and a T-38 from Holloman. Visible inside the gun bays are the Pontiac M-39A 20 mm cannon, the disconnected ammunition feed guides and the silver ammo box that holds 280 rounds per gun (*Minert*)

Opposite above This 65th AS F-5 wears yet another variation of the 'new lizard' camouflage, 57th FWW 'WA' tail codes and silhouette insignia. Freshly painted, s/n 73–0885 was a recent acquisition from the 405th TTW at Luke when photographed in June 1988 (*Rogers*)

Opposite below The USAF's largest F-5 unit, and the first to receive E-models (June 1973), was the 425th TFTS, 58th TFTW at Williams AFB, Arizona. They flew most of their Tigers in an anodized-silver finish, but only a few all-silver birds flew with the Nellis aggressors. The 'Bort' number on this F-5, s/n 72-1388, is non-standard, as is the lack of national insignia (*Knowles*)

Above In July 1989, 'blue 65', the mount of Lt Col Mike Koerner, the last commander of the 65th AS, was mounted on a pedestal in full camouflage and bogus 57th FWW markings as a reminder of the F-5 aggressor era at Nellis

Fourth generation aggressor

'Red 02', with Lt 'Johnny B' Good at the controls, taxies out past Miramar's famed Hangar One and a line-up of Top Gun and 'Bandit' A-4s. Because of VF-126's proximity to Top Gun (they share the same two-hangar complex and ramp), they often assist in developing and testing NFWS training scenarios

Above Grrrr! Lt Bruce 'Puppy' Fecht obliges with the aggressor growl

Left Wearing his distinctive flight suit, Top Gun's current boss, Capt Bud 'Thunder' Taylor, straps into his TF-16N. Top Gun pilots also wear special brown leather name tags

Left In 1987, Top Gun's fleet of ageing F-5s was phased out and replaced by a dozen brand-new F-16Ns, perhaps the hottest US fighter around. The Navy's Falcons feature several modifications that make them different from Air Force F-16s. Foremost is the new GE F110-100 engine. In addition, the hulking M61A-1 cannon has been removed and the powerful, but heavy, Westinghouse pulse-doppler radar replaced with a lighter model. This Miramar line-up shows the blue/grey camouflage, standard on the F-16N

Below The home of the Pacific Fleet Adversary Squadron. Officially known as VF-126 'Bandits', 'Fighting 126' shares the Miramar ramp with the NFWS. A one-time attack RAG (replacement air group), VF-126 was designated a fighter squadron in October 1965 and began flying TA-4Fs in April 1967. Three years later they received their first A-4Es and the aggressor mission that they still fly today

Above The next generation. One of VF-45's ten F-16Ns decked out in the Navy's standard Falcon camouflage and wearing red 'Bort' numbers on the nose and large Soviet stars on the tail (*Trombecky*)

Opposite above One of six VF-45 Falcons on loan to VF-43 during most of 1988/89. It was photographed at NAS Cecil Field whilst on detachment to provide adversary training to VF-101 and VFA-106, the East Coast F-14 and F/A-18 FRSs (fleet replacement squadrons). It carries typical 'armament' for a mission in the TACTS: a blue dummy AIM-9L Sidewinder on the starboard wingtip and an orange ACMI data pod on the port side (*Michaels*)

Opposite below This VF-45 Falcon represents half the Navy's East Coast TF-16N strength. Like Top Gun, the 'Blackbirds' use their two-seaters for familiarization flights and conversion training

Unlike VF-43, which camouflaged its Rockwell T-2C Buckeyes, VF-126 kept their aircraft in the standard white and orange training colours. These portly two-seaters are used to train Top Gun students in the art of recovering from a flatspin, a predicament which has claimed the lives of many F-14 crews over the years

And now the bad news. The 64th AS commander, Lt Col Mike Scott, confirms that the end is near for the last of the Nellis aggressor squadrons. Because of impending cuts in the FY91 defense budget, the 64th AS has now been deactivated

Overleaf Unlike the camouflage on an actual MiG-23, the 64th AS brown and green *'Flogger'* scheme is applied in a wrap-around pattern

Left As of September 1989, the 64th AS was flying only two F-16s in the *'Flogger'* scheme, s/n 86–251 and 86–272

Above Checks completed, an aggressor jock prepares to taxi out for another ACM sortie. The reaction of USAF pilots to the addition of the F-16 to aggressor squadron rosters was the same as that of the Navy pilots: 'We hate to see the F-5s go, but for what we're getting in return it's worth it. We used to be at a disadvantage going against most fighters in the F-5, but not any more. Now that we're all equal, it's a more realistic free-for-all without all the restrictive engagement rules we used to have to allow the F-5 to keep up'

With the retirement of the F-5 from service in April 1989, the Air Force aggressor squadrons stepped up to F-16 Fighting Falcons. At Nellis, the 65th AS was deactivated and over the course of the year, the 64th took delivery of 18 brand-new F-16Cs. The first of them, s/n 87–317, wore a factory applied white and mint-green camouflage based on that of the MiG-29 *Fulcrum*

Above Line-up of the 'new' 64th AS Aggressors at Nellis, July 1989

Right The USAF aggressor pilots flew as much as they could before the pending disbandment came into effect. Surrounded by fellow 'Soviet' Falcons, the pilot of 'red 69' commences his firing up sequence

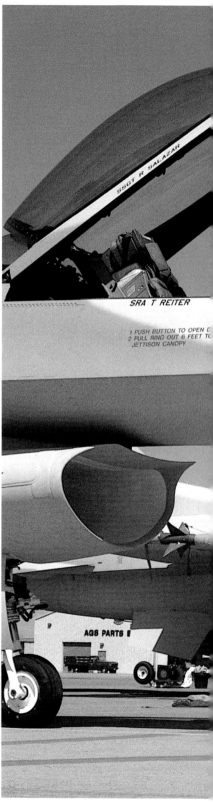

Above The excellent finish of the paint on these new F-16s is clearly visible in this close up tail shot

Right Groundcrew watch as 'red 69' completes engine run-up checks. Though the difference is barely noticeable, s/n 86–269 wears the MiG-29 scheme with medium-grey instead of mint-green over white

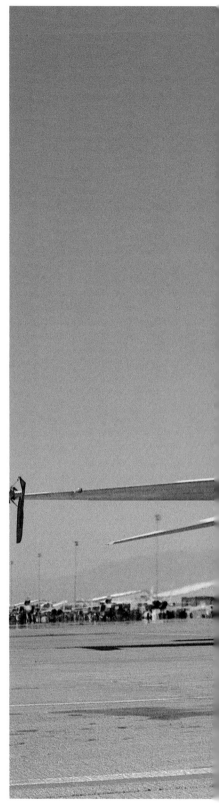

The Israeli connection

In 1986, VF-43 made naval history of sorts when it became the first aggressor squadron to employ foreign-built aircraft in the adversary role. Twelve Israeli Kfirs (Navy designation F-21A) were obtained on a one-year lease from Israel to supplement VF-43's A-4, F-5 and T-38 fleet. A direct descendant of the French Mirage 5, the F-21 has a performance envelope comparable to that of the MiG-21 and -23, and has developed a reputation for outstanding ruggedness and reliability

Overleaf This F-21 carries fuel tanks still painted in Israeli sand and stone desert camouflage. The only other dash of colour in VF-43's drab scheme is the unit badge on the tail; a mailed-fist on a blue and red crest crushing a Soviet MiG-17 in its grip. After VF-43's leased Kfirs were returned to Israel, their strength was supplemented by six F-16Ns on loan from VF-45 (*James*)

Above Capt Dick Thomas, the 'Snipers' intelligence officer, in the cockpit of 'red 13'

Right A four-ship of VF-43 aggressors off the Virginia coast in September 1984. From the bottom of the stack, LCDR Gene 'Geno' Garrett in 'Ambush 12', an F-21A Kfir; LCDR Curt 'Potsie' Francis in 'Ambush 23', an A-4E; LCDR Mike 'Rex' Orr in 'Ambush' 42', a TA-4J; and one of the very first female aggressors, Lt Linda 'Peaches' Schaffer in 'Ambush 31', a T-2C (*Trombecky*)

Right From any angle, it's easy to see the Kfir's resemblance to its French progenitors, the Mirage IIICJ and the Mirage 5. The most obvious differences between them are the dorsal fin air intake, the fixed, sweptback canards above the engine intakes and the miniature strakes at the very tip of the nose

Below The only Marine Corps squadron dedicated exclusively to adversary training, VMFT-401 flew the Israeli Aircraft Industries (IAI) F-21A Kfir (Israeli designation C-2) since the unit was formed in 1987. Six of its 13 Kfirs were painted in the same grey air superiority scheme popularized by VF-43. Major 'Boot' Sadler, wearing a Top Gun instructor's patch, taxies out for a mission in March 1988

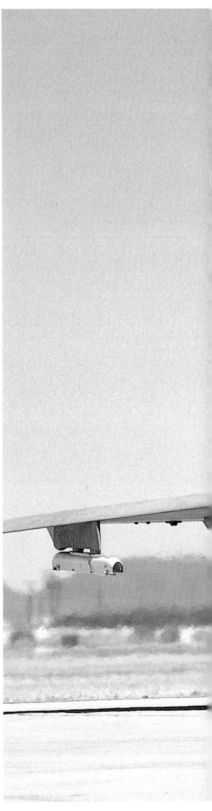

Above Capt Joel 'Molokai' Hagenbrock poses next to his Kfir, which is assigned the temporary bureau number 999794. He swears this picture was for his mother, not for his 'I-love-me' wall in his den

Left With civilian groundcrew ready to assist, a 'Sniper' climbs down from his Kfir after a mission in the El Centro ranges, only 100 flying miles northwest of Yuma. The telltale sign of a TACTS mission, the orange ACMI pod, is mounted on the right wing pylon

Above Another provision of the agreement with Israel was that IAI personnel supervise the maintenance of the Kfirs during the length of the lease. So, 18 Israelis and some 80 US civilians employed by Israeli Aircraft Services (IAS) spent three years on contract in the southern Arizona desert. Here, an IAS mechanic repacks a Kfir's brake chute after a sortie

Left The F-21, like the exotic SR-71 Blackbird, was a notorious fuel leaker on the ground – so bad, in fact, that a 55-gallon drum on wheels was a required piece of ground support equipment. It was placed under the lowest point of the internal belly tank

Left A Kfir's General Electric J79-GE-17 turbojet is air-started, the red oil drum remaining in place to catch leaking fuel. Outstanding contract maintenance and the Kfir's rugged construction resulted in a 99 per cent mission-readiness rate, enabling VMFT-401's 13 aircraft to average nearly 400 ACM sorties per month

Below Ready for an early morning take-off at Yuma

Opposite above Ubiquitous drum strategically positioned, a storeless F-21 is plugged into the power cart before engine spool up. The VF-43 scheme used on most VMFT-401 Kfirs proved very suitable for ACM over the Yuma ranges

Opposite below All systems go, Capt Thomas taxies out with the hood slightly ajar to help him keep cool in the boiling Arizona sun. Rearward vision is rather limited in the F-21, a definite drawback when it comes to tight ACM

Above Olive-green replaces the usual mint-green in this variation of the Israeli 'sand and stone' camouflage worn by 'red 05', BuNo 99705, at Yuma in May 1989. Because of the contract maintenance situation, the 'Snipers' staged almost exclusively out of Yuma, often flying their adversary training sorties alongside Yuma-based MAWTS-1 (Marine Aviation Weapons and Tactics Squadron One). The average ACM mission in the Kfir lasted an hour and ten minutes. The VMFT-401 Kfirs flew their last mission at Yuma on 24 September 1989 and, contrary to rumours that they were to be sold on the civilian market by an ex-military-jet broker in Reno, were promptly flown to NAS Norfolk, where the IAI team disassembled them for shipment back to Israel in the last week of October 1989

'Soviet' Hueys

Left Often overlooked because it flies helicopters instead of jet fighters, the US Army has an aggressor unit of its own: 'C' Company, 3/195th Assault Helicopter Battalion. Based in California at Barstow-Daggett Airport, the 'Desert Hawks' fly four modified Bell UH-1 Hueys in support of the National Training Center (NTC) at Fort Irwin. Unlike other aggressor units, the 'Desert Hawks' wear full size Soviet stars in addition to yellow 'Bort' numbers and 'danger' warnings in Cyrillic on the rear rotor

Below The 'Desert Hawks' fly some of the oldest helicopters still in active Army service. The white number '928' on the nose is the only clue to 'yellow 01's' true identity: UH-1D, s/n 66–0928. 'Yellow 02' is also a D model, while '03' is a C model, s/n 66–15223, and '04' is an H model, s/n 69–15855. One of the Multiple Integrated Laser Engagement System (MILES) sensors is visible strapped across the nose of the Huey

Left During preflight, a crewmember checks the sighting device for the UH-1's MILES. Both the helicopter and the 'enemy' vehicles it is hunting are equipped with a sight, a laser transmitter and numerous sensors. After aiming and firing, a hit is indicated by a flashing light on the target and a confirmation signal received by a monitor panel aboard the 'shooter'. Depending on the rules of engagement, a confirmed 'kill' can take the victim out of action permanently, or for only a few minutes

Above As CW-2 Bill Sexton brings 'yellow 04' up over a ridge behind a column of 'enemy' tanks, co-pilot/gunner CW-4 Bill Butts reaches for the MILES sight stowed above his head

As the gunner in '04' takes aim, 'yellow 01' in the background fires off one of its pylon-mounted flares, simulating the launch of a laser-guided AT-6 'Spiral' missile. Then, barely 50 feet off the deck, he banks hard left to avoid defensive fire. Though the heavily-armed *Hind* gunship is not very fast or manoeuvrable, Army aggressor pilots complain that the tired old Hueys are even slower and less manoeuvrable, and make for a very poor *Hind* simulator. There was some hope that the Sikorsky H-19/S-55s being converted to *Hind-E* look alikes by Orlando Helicopter Airways would solve the problem, but when the company went bankrupt, so did dreams of a better *Hind*

Left Mounted inboard on the port rocket launcher is the MILES laser transmitter; inboard on the starboard side is the high-intensity light that flashes on when the helicopter has been 'killed' by groundfire

Below Another modification to these aggressor Hueys is a fibreglass shell mounted on the nose to simulate the *Hind's* forward observer cockpit and chin turret. MILES sensors are strapped across the nose, above and below the sliding passenger doors, and along the length of the tail

Left Operating from a forward base between two ridgelines, a pair of 'Desert Hawks' demonstrate that their simulated *Hind* camouflage is extremely effective in the sand and scrub environment of the Fort Irwin range

Above The classic tank-killing team. As an aggressor UH-1 waits in the 'penalty box' after being downed by groundfire, an A-10 wheels around to finish off the job

Above The Hueys have received several cosmetic changes in the vain attempt to make them look more like Mil Mi-24s. One of these modifications is the addition of three-point rocket launchers to simulate the *Hind's* large lifting wings and rocket pods. These rocket launchers never carry anything more than flares that are fired off in flight to simulate rockets being launched

Right 'Yellow 01' returns from an attack mission at Fort Irwin, a 15-minute hop across the desert from Barstow-Daggett. It's not unusual for the helicopters to be 'shot down' several times on a sortie, only to land, re-arm and return to the fight as a 'new' aggressor

The real thing

Left In March 1988, the Defense Test and Support Evaluation Agency (DTESA), at the direction of the Pentagon's Operational Test and Evaluation (OT&E) office, began purchasing ex-Soviet aircraft from Combat Core Certification Professionals of Reno, Nevada. The aircraft, ex-Chinese and Polish MiG-15s, MiG-17s, MiG-19s, MiG-21s, Il-14s, An-2s and a Mil Mi-2 helicopter, as well as Soviet communications and air defence equipment, were acquired for threat simulation and evaluation as part of the Defense Department's 'Capability Improvement Program'. After use in a three-week mobile threat test at Kirtland AFB, New Mexico, in September 1988, most of the DTESA fleet is now in open storage there

Below One of DTESA's reserve MiG-21F *Fishbeds*, currently in storage at Al Reddick's 'CIA Air' in Reno, Nevada. At least two other ex-Polish Air Force MiG-21s are hangared at DTESA's facility at Kirtland AFB, New Mexico

Opposite above Slightly larger and faster than its predecessor, the MiG-17 was flown by the air forces of some 25 countries and was license-built in Poland, China and Czechoslovakia. This version of the MiG-17PF *Fresco* C is either a Polish-built Mielec LIM-5P or a Chinese Shenyang F-4. At any rate, it is the limited all-weather fighter version of the MiG-17 and carries the *Izumrud* AI radar in the extended housing in the nose

Opposite below Designed in 1947 and operational in 1949, the MiG-15 was a crude, but effective first-generation jet fighter that made its name in the Korean War. This stubby little MiG-15UTI *Midget* (actually a Polish-built LIM-3 or a Chinese Shenyang FT-5) is the two-seat trainer version of the *Fagot*. Considered obsolete 25 years ago, its role with DTESA is unknown

Above Except for the natural metal MiG-21s, DTESA's entire MiG fleet wears this unusual scheme of light grey and Prussian blue. All wear a red three-digit 'Bort' number and the DTESA emblem on the tail. Here, a MiG-17F *Fresco* complete with underwing fuel tanks sits amongst other ex-eastern bloc hardware. As all of DTESA's aggressor fleet are ex-Chinese and Polish machines, it's more accurate to call this a Mielec LIM-5 or a Shenyang F-4

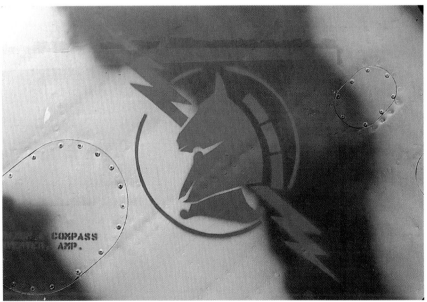

Above DTESA's Mil Mi-2 *Hoplite* helicopter. Though the prototype was designed and built by the Soviet Mil bureau in 1962, all production helicopters were actually built in Poland by PZL starting in 1965

Left DTESA's distinctive 'trojan horse' emblem which adorns all of its aircraft